Charles Lindbergh

A Photo-Illustrated Biography
by Lucile Davis

Consultant:
Marlene K. White
The Charles A. and Anne Morrow Lindbergh Foundation

Bridgestone Books

an imprint of Capstone Press
Mankato, Minnesota

Bridgestone Books are published by Capstone Press
151 Good Counsel Drive, P.O. Box 669, Mankato, Minnesota 56002
http://www.capstonepress.com

Library of Congress Cataloging-in-Publication Data
Davis, Lucile.
    Charles Lindbergh: a photo-illustrated biography/by Lucile Davis.
    p. cm.—(Photo-illustrated biographies)
    Includes bibliographical references (p. 23).
    Summary: A biography of the aviator and environmental activist who became the first
person to fly nonstop across the Atlantic Ocean.
    ISBN 0-7368-3430-3 (softcover) ISBN 0-7368-0204-5 (hardcover)
    1. Lindbergh, Charles A. (Charles Augustus), 1902–1974—Juvenile literature. 2. Lindbergh,
Charles A. (Charles Augustus), 1902–1974—Pictorial works—Juvenile literature. 3. Air pilots—
United States—Biography—Juvenile literature. [1. Lindbergh, Charles A. (Charles Augustus),
1902–1974. 2. Air pilots.] I. Title. II. Series.
TL540.L5D38 1999
629.13'092—dc21
[B]   98-31473
                                                                                          CIP
                                                                                          AC

Editorial Credits
Chuck Miller, editor; Timothy Halldin, cover designer and illustrator; Kimberly Danger,
    photo researcher

Photo Credits
Corbis/Minnesota Historical Society, 10
Corbis-Bettmann, 4, 8, 14, 16, 18, 20
Spectrum Graphics, 6
UPI/Corbis-Bettmann, cover

Table of Contents

"I learned that danger was a part of life not always to be shunned. It often surrounded the things you liked most to do."
—Charles describing his flight from New York to Paris in his book *The Spirit of St. Louis*

American Hero

In 1927, Charles Lindbergh became the first person to fly across the Atlantic Ocean alone. Charles flew the *Spirit of St. Louis* from New York to Paris, France. Today, his airplane hangs in the Smithsonian National Air and Space Museum in Washington, D.C.

Charles stood up for many of his beliefs. Charles said the United States should stay out of World War II (1939–1945). But Charles helped win the war when the United States entered it.

Charles was an inventor. He helped develop the world's first heart pump. He also helped create the U.S. space program. Charles' ideas helped the space program land a man on the moon safely.

Charles was an environmentalist. He worked with the World Wildlife Fund to protect rare animals. Charles also traveled the world to visit native peoples. He respected their ways of life.

Charles was a pilot, an inventor, and an environmentalist.

Early Years

Charles was born February 4, 1902, in Detroit, Michigan. His father, Charles Augustus Lindbergh Sr., was a lawyer in Little Falls, Minnesota. His mother, Evangeline Land Lindbergh, was a high school science teacher there.

Charles Sr. was elected to the U.S. Congress in 1906. The family lived in Washington, D.C., part of the year. During spring and summer, Charles and his mother lived on a small farm near Little Falls.

Charles attended many different schools because his family moved often. Evangeline helped Charles with his homework so he would not get behind. Charles Sr. taught Charles to camp, swim, and canoe. He taught Charles to depend on himself.

From an early age, Charles dreamed of flying. He watched airplanes fly over the house in Little Falls. He read about airplanes every chance he could.

Charles lived in Washington, D.C., while his father was serving in the U.S. Congress.

Learning to Fly

Charles attended college after he graduated from high school in 1918. He went to the University of Wisconsin in Madison, Wisconsin. After two years, Charles quit. He wanted to fly airplanes.

In 1922, Charles began working at an airplane factory in Lincoln, Nebraska. He took flying lessons from one of the workers there.

Charles spent the summer on a barnstorming tour. Barnstormers flew their airplanes to cities and towns across North America. They charged people for airplane rides. Some barnstormers did tricks like wingwalking. A barnstormer walked on the wings of an airplane as it flew.

At first, Charles worked as a mechanic on a barnstorming tour. He fixed airplanes and filled them with gas. Later, Charles learned to wingwalk. Charles was flying airplanes by the end of the tour.

Charles (left) learned to fly as a barnstormer. He also learned how to fix mechanical problems on airplanes.

"A pilot can't fly at all without taking some risk."
—Charles in his book *The Spirit of St. Louis*

A Pilot

Charles joined the United States Army Air Service in 1924. He trained to be a pilot at Brooks Field in San Antonio, Texas. More than 100 students started training with him. Only 19 finished. Charles graduated with the best grades in his class.

The U.S. Army placed Charles in the Air Service Reserve Corps in 1925. The United States was not at war. The army did not need many pilots.

In 1926, Charles took a job with the Robertson Aircraft Company. The company had just started flying mail. Charles became the chief pilot. He flew mail from St. Louis, Missouri, to Chicago, Illinois.

Flying the mail was a dangerous job. Charles and other pilots depended on eyesight to fly their airplanes. Bad weather forced Charles to make many parachute jumps. But the parachute carried him safely to the ground each time.

Bad weather often caused Charles (third from left) and other pilots to crash their airplanes.

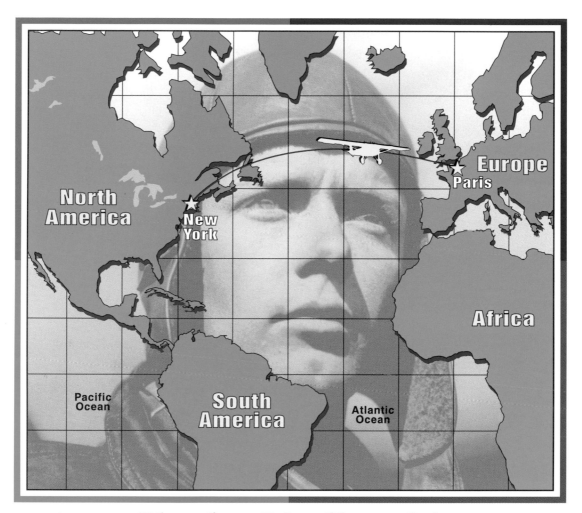

Charles Lindbergh's
1927 Transatlantic Flight

A Challenge

In 1919, a New York businessman gave pilots around the world a challenge. Raymond Orteig offered $25,000 to the first pilot to fly nonstop from New York to Paris, France. No pilot had been able to do it. In 1926, Charles began planning his flight.

Other pilots also were planning flights across the Atlantic Ocean. They had copilots and big airplanes. Charles planned to fly alone with a small airplane. Businessmen from St. Louis helped Charles pay for the airplane. They named it the *Spirit of St. Louis*.

By May 20, 1927, Charles and his airplane were ready. The other pilots and their airplanes were not.

Charles took off for Paris early that morning. He had not slept much the night before. He would have to stay awake for the next 33 1/2 hours. Charles flew through rain and ice storms. He landed in Paris the next night. People considered Charles to be a hero.

Charles designed the *Spirit of St. Louis* himself. Workers at an airplane factory in San Diego, California, built the airplane.

Fame

President Calvin Coolidge wanted Charles to return to the United States right away. He sent a navy ship called the *U.S.S. Memphis* to France to get Charles.

Charles arrived in Washington, D.C., on June 10, 1927. President Coolidge awarded Charles the Distinguished Flying Cross. Three days later, a parade in New York honored Charles. Four million people came to see him.

Charles flew to many U.S. cities and foreign countries. He used his fame to help promote flying. Charles said airplanes could be used for travel. In Mexico, Charles met the U.S. ambassador to Mexico, Dwight Whitney Morrow, and his family. Charles fell in love with the ambassador's daughter, Anne.

Anne and Charles married on May 27, 1929. Charles taught Anne how to fly. Charles and Anne mapped airplane routes for airlines.

Charles taught Anne how to fly. Anne was the radio operator on most flights.

The Kidnapping

In 1932, Charles and Anne moved to the small town of Hopewell, New Jersey. They hoped to find privacy for their one and a half-year-old son, Charles Jr.

But Charles Jr. was kidnapped one month after the Lindberghs moved to Hopewell. Ten weeks later, searchers found him dead in the woods outside the Lindbergh home.

Police looked for the killer for two years. In 1934, police arrested Bruno Hauptmann for the kidnapping and murder of Charles Jr. Many people called the trial of Bruno Hauptmann "The Trial of the Century." A jury found Hauptmann guilty.

Charles and Anne moved to England after the trial. They wanted to keep their second son, Jon, safe. Charles and Anne had four more children. Land, Anne, Scott, and Reeve Lindbergh were born between 1937 and 1945.

News reporters invaded the town of Hopewell, New Jersey, during the kidnapping trial. "The Trial of the Century" lasted six weeks.

"We have contributed the best we could give to our country in time of peace. Now, we must contribute the best we can in time of war."
—Charles in a letter to America First supporters

World War II

Charles was no longer a member of the Air Service Reserve Corps. But the U.S. Army wanted him to help strengthen its air force. In 1939, the Lindberghs returned to the United States.

Charles opposed World War II. He gave speeches saying the United States should stay out of the war.

Charles stopped giving the speeches when the United States entered World War II in 1941. Instead, he worked hard to help the United States win the war. He served as a test pilot for new airplanes and flew combat missions.

Many people did not like Charles' views about World War II. But Charles helped the United States win the war. President Dwight Eisenhower made Charles a brigadier general in the U.S. Air Force after the war.

Charles gave many speeches at America First meetings. This group thought the United States should stay out of World War II.

"I realized that if I had to choose,
I would rather have birds than airplanes."
—Charles talking about his concern for
air pollution caused by airplanes

Losing a Hero

Charles noticed the world's environment was in danger. New inventions like airplanes improved people's lives. But these inventions also caused pollution that hurt people and the land, sea, and air.

In 1962, he traveled to Africa to live with the Masai tribe. He was concerned about the effects new inventions had on native peoples. Charles wanted others to respect the Masai's way of life.

Charles helped the World Wildlife Fund. He worked to protect animals such as blue whales and humpback whales.

In 1972, Charles became sick with cancer. Two years later, Charles and Anne flew to Maui, Hawaii. He and Anne owned a house there.

Charles planned his own funeral when they landed. He died one week later on August 26, 1974. The world had lost a hero.

Charles worked to reduce the effects of new inventions on the earth's environment.

Fast Facts about Charles Lindbergh

 Charles won a Pulitzer Prize for his book *The Spirit of St. Louis.* It is one of the highest awards an author can receive.

 Charles also was awarded the Medal of Honor by the U.S. Congress for his nonstop flight across the Atlantic Ocean.

 Charles was a civilian test pilot during World War II. But he flew 50 combat missions for the U.S. Army during the war.

Dates in Charles Lindbergh's Life

1902—Born February 4 in Detroit, Michigan
1918—Graduates from high school
1924—Joins the U.S. Army Air Service
1926—Flies mail for Robertson Aircraft Company
1927—Becomes the first person to fly nonstop from New York to Paris
1929—Marries Anne Morrow
1932—Charles' son, Charles Jr., is kidnapped and murdered
1935—Moves to England with his family
1939—Moves back to the United States; helps with the U.S. war effort
1962—Lives with the Masai tribe in Africa
1974—Dies on August 26 in Hawaii

Words to Know

airplane route (AIR-plane ROOT)—the path a pilot flies to get from one place to another

ambassador (am-BASS-uh-dur)—a person sent by a government to represent it in another country

barnstorming (BARN-storm-ing)—flying to entertain people; barnstormers charged money for rides and performed tricks for people.

environment (en-VYE-ruhn-muhnt)—the land, sea, and air; Charles worked to protect the environment from pollution.

parachute (PA-ruh-shoot)—a large piece of strong, light cloth; a parachute allows a person to jump from a high place and float safely to the ground.

pilot (PYE-luht)—a person who flies an airplane

Read More

Burleigh, Robert. *Flight.* New York: Philomel Books, 1991.

Giblin, James. *Charles A. Lindbergh: A Human Hero.* New York: Clarion Books, 1997.

Stein, R. Conrad. *The Spirit of St. Louis.* Cornerstones of Freedom. Chicago: Children's Press, 1994.

Taylor, Richard L. *The First Solo Transatlantic Flight: The Story of Charles Lindbergh and His Airplane, the Spirit of St. Louis.* A First Book. New York: Franklin Watts, 1995.

Useful Addresses

Charles A. Lindbergh House
Route 3
Box 245
Lindbergh Drive
Little Falls, MN 56345

**The Charles A. and Anne
    Morrow Lindbergh Foundation**
708 South 3rd Street
Suite 110
Minneapolis, MN 55415

Internet Sites

Charles Lindbergh
http://www.CharlesLindbergh.com
The Lindberg Foundation
http://www.lindberghfoundation.org/index.html
National Aviation Hall of Fame: Charles Augustus Lindbergh
http://www.nationalaviation.org/enshrinee/lindberghch.html

Index